FOR PETER

✠

Lives and Legends of the Saints
Copyright © Frances Lincoln Limited 1995
Text copyright © Frances Lincoln 1995

For photographic acknowledgements
and copyright details, see pages 42-45

First published in Great Britain in 1995
by Frances Lincoln Limited, 4 Torriano Mews
Torriano Avenue, London NW5 2RZ

British Library
Cataloguing in Publication Data
available on request

ISBN 0-7112-0976-6

Set in Perpetua

Printed and bound in Hong Kong

1 3 5 7 9 8 6 4 2

LIVES and LEGENDS ✠ of the ✠ SAINTS

With paintings from
the great art museums
of the world

✠

CAROLE ARMSTRONG

FRANCES LINCOLN

AUTHOR'S NOTE

IN the early days of Christianity, Paul used the term 'saints' to describe all his fellow Christians. Later, as more people were converted to the faith, the Church decided to award the title of 'Saint' to martyrs - men or women who chose to die rather than renounce their faith - to miracle-workers, and to the first monks, who gave up family life to serve Christ.

Saints in painting are traditionally portrayed with haloes - blazing circles of light around or behind their heads. Even when they are not named, they can often be identified by their symbols - objects or emblems connected with their lives or legends. Saint Michael, for example, holds a pair of scales to weigh the souls of men and women and Saint Lucy carries a pair of eyes on a handle or a plate.

While some of the saints in this book are remembered for their courageous lives and others for the legends woven around them, all have inspired the world's great artists to commemorate them gloriously in painting.

✠

CONTENTS

DOROTHY

 THE legendary Dorothy of Cappadocia was a 3rd-century Christian renowned for her beauty and her religious devotion. Hearing of her, the Roman governor of the province sent two sisters who had renounced Christianity to persuade her to give up her faith. Instead, Dorothy converted them back to Christianity again! This infuriated the governor and, ordering the sisters to be burned alive, he forced Dorothy to witness their sufferings. As Dorothy watched, she prayed for the women. The governor then commanded her to be tortured on a rack and executed.

As Dorothy was led to her death, a young lawyer called Theophilus jeered and mockingly asked her to send him flowers and fruit when she reached heaven. Dorothy replied that she would - and it is said that an angel appeared to Theophilus disguised as a young boy, carrying apples and roses wrapped in linen. Theophilus was astonished, for it was the middle of winter when no flowers could possibly bloom. He became a Christian, and later he too died for his faith.

In this painting, part of an altarpiece, the artist has posed Dorothy against a damask and gold cloth painted in fine detail, and has made her skin almost as white as her dress to emphasise her innocence. The red rose in her hand is a symbol of her martyrdom. Dorothy is often shown carrying a basket of heavenly fruit and flowers.

JOHN the BAPTIST

ELISABETH, cousin to the Virgin Mary, was past the age of child-bearing when an angel visited her husband, Zacharias, to tell him that they would have a son called John who would be a great prophet and holy man.

This prediction was fulfilled, for when John grew up he lived the life of a hermit in the desert of Judaea, wearing only animal skins, eating wild honey and locusts and preaching repentance to his fellow men. He offered to wash their sins away by baptising them in the River Jordan, and told them that someone else was coming who would baptise them, not with water, but with the Holy Spirit. It was John who baptised Jesus and proclaimed him to be the Messiah, the 'Lamb of God'.

But one day, John denounced Herod Antipas, the Governor of Galilee, for marrying Herodias, his half-brother's wife - and immediately John was thrown into prison. Herodias had a daughter called Salomé who was renowned for her graceful dancing. When she danced at Herod's birthday feast, he was so delighted that he offered her anything she wanted as a gift. Unfortunately, Salomé's mother persuaded her to ask for the head of John the Baptist. John was executed, and his head was presented to Salomé on a plate.

John the Baptist, painted here by Bosch, is wearing rich red robes and meditating in an eerie landscape, surrounded by strange plants symbolising evil. John points to a lamb, which is his symbol.

MICHAEL

MICHAEL, whose name means 'like God', is an archangel, a soldier of heaven and a special messenger from God to man. In the Scriptures, he is described as the protector of Israel, a prince of the heavenly host and one of four archangels who hold up God's throne. The Book of Revelations tells how Michael and his angels overcome the Devil and his angels - hence the many paintings portraying Michael as a handsome warrior carrying a sword and killing a serpent, a dragon or a demon, all symbols of the Devil.

In Crivelli's picture, part of an altarpiece, Michael wears dazzling armour encrusted with precious jewels. His wings are rainbow-coloured and splendid lions are painted on his leg armour.

The scales Michael carries show his power, for he can weigh the souls of men and women and rescue them even from the jaws of hell. His feast day at the end of September is known as Michaelmas.

✠ 12

MARY MAGDALEN

PATRON SAINT of THOSE WHO FOLLOW
the CONTEMPLATIVE LIFE, LADIES'
HAIRDRESSERS and REPENTANT SINNERS

 **MARY** Magdalen became a devout follower of Jesus after he cured her of an illness caused by seven devils. Saint Luke's Gospel tells how she lovingly washed Jesus' feet with her tears, drying them with her long hair and pouring scented ointment over them.

Mary was at the Crucifixion and two days later she went to see the tomb where Jesus was buried. When she found it empty, she wept, and while she was crying Jesus appeared to her. At first Mary did not recognise him - but then he spoke, and asked her to tell the other disciples he would soon ascend into heaven.

Mary later travelled to France and converted many people to Christianity, spending the last thirty years of her life alone in the desert, where it is said she was fed by angels.

In this painting by Memlinc, Mary holds her symbol, a pot of ointment.

✠ 13

MARTIN of TOURS

PATRON SAINT of FRANCE, BEGGARS and SOLDIERS

DURING the Middle Ages, one of the most popular saints was Martin. He was born in Hungary during the reign of Constantine the Great, and as a young boy he became a Christian and ran away to join a monastery. But his father, an officer in the imperial army, forced his son to become a soldier too, and soon Martin was serving as a cavalry officer in France.

One freezing winter's day, outside the gates of Amiens, Martin saw a poor, almost naked beggar shivering with cold. Taking his sword, Martin cut his own cloak in half and gave one half to the beggar. That night, Martin dreamt that Christ appeared to him wearing the piece of cloak he had given away.

Martin became a monk and from that time onward devoted his life to preaching and performing miracles. It is said that when Church officials came to ask him to become Bishop of Tours, a position he did not want, he hid, but his hiding-place was given away by a honking goose!

In this fresco, the Roman military leader is astonished to see Martin abandoning his career as a soldier. The detailed way in which the artist Martini has painted the horses, tents, lances and banners, and the clothes of the military leaders, tells us much about the Roman army - even down to the soldier standing behind Martin who is being paid for his services. Martin's symbol is a goose or a globe of fire, which was said to appear over the saint's head when he prayed.

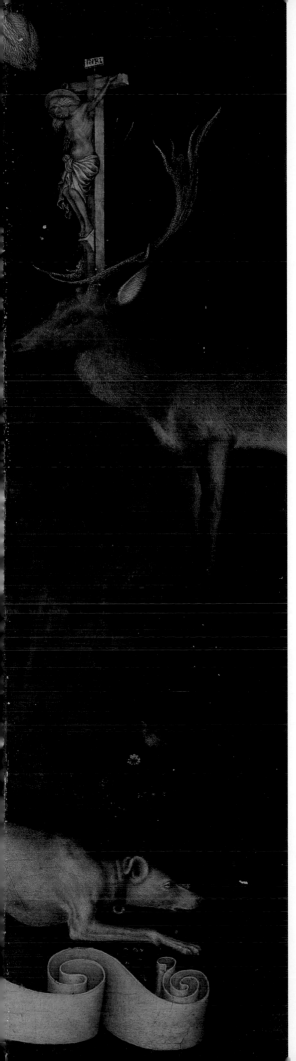

EUSTACE

PATRON SAINT of HUNTSMEN

EUSTACE was a powerful Roman general living in the reign of the emperor Trajan. One day, while out hunting, he had a glorious vision: before him stood a magnificent stag, a crucifix glimmering between its antlers. Then and there, Eustace decided to become a Christian. But when his faith was discovered, he was thrown out of the army and lost his fortune. Worse still, his sons were carried off by wild beasts and his wife was kidnapped by pirates.

Years passed. A military crisis arose and Eustace was recalled to deal with it. He was reunited with his wife and sons, who by some miracle had survived. All went well, for a while. But eventually he was ordered to show his allegiance by sacrificing to the Roman gods. Eustace refused - so he and his family were roasted to death inside a bronze bull.

Pisanello uses this legend to paint a landscape full of realistic birds and animals against a strongly patterned, tapestry-like background. He paints the animals in different sizes, and the trees and rocks are not drawn to scale - giving the painting a fairy-tale quality. Eustace's symbol is a stag with a cross between its horns.

✱ 17

LUCY

LUCY was a wealthy Sicilian noblewoman living in Syracuse in the 3rd century. She was wooed by many suitors, including one who became so passionate about the beauty of her eyes, he could not sleep. Lucy, fearing that he would always be unhappy, tore out her eyes and sent them to him on a plate. He was so inspired by her courage and devotion to Christianity that he too became a Christian. Lucy's eyes and sight were miraculously restored, and she became the patron saint of sight. In Sweden, her feast day is celebrated as a festival of light; there and in Sicily, the song 'Santa Lucia' is sung in her praise.

The artist Cossa paints Lucy with a magnificent golden halo, wearing the rich robes of a noblewoman. She carries a palm leaf, a symbol of her triumph over death, and holds a pair of eyes set on an elegant handle, which refers to the famous episode in her life. In some paintings she appears holding a lamp to suggest divine wisdom, or with her neck or hands pierced by a dagger - the weapon that finally killed her. The angle of the figure and the way she is gazing downwards suggest that this elegant painting was probably placed high above a church altar.

ANDREW
PATRON SAINT of GREECE, RUSSIA, SCOTLAND and FISHERMEN

PETER
PATRON SAINT of FISHERMEN

ANDREW and Simon were brothers working as fishermen near the Sea of Galilee and became the first two disciples of Jesus. He called them 'fishers of men' and named Simon *Kephas* or Peter, meaning 'rock'.

Andrew took part in Jesus' most famous miracle – feeding five thousand people with five loaves and two fishes. After the Resurrection, Andrew became a famous preacher, but was eventually captured and crucified on an X-shaped cross (his symbol), on which he is said to have preached to the people for two days before he died. His other symbol is a fishing-net.

Peter is remembered for three times denying his association with Jesus, and later for three times confirming his loyalty to his master. He became the foremost apostle and the greatest miracle-worker of the Christian Church. Tradition says that eventually the emperor Nero sentenced him to be crucified upside-down. Peter's symbol is two crossed keys, for he is thought to guard the gates of the kingdom of heaven.

This scene is one of ten cartoons – full size watercolours – which the artist Raphael was commissioned to paint as tapestry designs for the Sistine Chapel in Rome. It portrays one of Jesus' great miracles. Peter, who is kneeling, and Andrew, standing behind him, look with amazement at Jesus, for, after a night in which the fisherman have caught nothing, he tells them to cast out their net once more – and when they pull it in, there are so many fish that the net breaks!

GEORGE

PATRON SAINT of ENGLAND, PORTUGAL, ARAGON,
GENOA, BOY SCOUTS, FARMERS, KNIGHTS and SOLDIERS

GEORGE came from a 2nd-century Christian family and grew up to be an officer in the Roman army. At that time, so the story goes, a dragon was terrorising a part of Libya and demanding human sacrifices. Villagers drew straws to determine the next victim, and one day the choice fell on a princess. She was dressed in her finest clothes and led to the dragon's lair.

Fortunately, George happened to be riding by on his white horse. After making the sign of the Cross, he attacked and wounded the dragon with his lance; then, drawing his sword, he beheaded the beast with a single blow. So inspired were the villagers by George's bravery that they all became Christians.

George's reputation grew during the Crusades when knights and soldiers chose him to represent Christian chivalry. He represents the triumph of good over evil, and is often shown with a red cross on his armour or his flag.

Raphael heightens the drama in this painting by linking all the figures with curving lines, so that our eyes travel from the dragon's arched neck up to George's billowing cloak, then across to the fluttering folds of the princess's gown.

FRANCIS of ASSISI

PATRON SAINT of ITALY, ANIMALS, BIRDS, ECOLOGISTS and MERCHANTS

FRANCIS of Assisi is one of the most greatly-loved saints, and both his life of extreme poverty and his affection for people and animals make him a favourite subject for artists. As a young man, he gave up his rich inheritance, choosing instead to lead a simple monastic life. He and his brown-robed friars were soon a familiar sight travelling from town to town begging for alms. They used the money to nurse lepers and the sick, and to rebuild ruined churches.

Many delightful stories are told about Francis. He is said to have called the sun 'Brother Sun', the moon 'Sister Moon', and his own body 'Brother Donkey'. He built the first Christmas crib. He tamed a fierce wolf. And it is said that on one occasion he preached so eloquently to the birds that they all gathered quietly to listen. Towards the end of his life, Francis had a vision of Christ and received the marks of Jesus' wounds, known as the *stigmata*, on his hands and feet.

Giotto painted the life of Francis many times, usually as frescoes decorating the walls of churches. In this picture, many different birds are gathered under a delicately painted tree to hear the saint preach. Francis' symbols include a wolf, a lamb, a lily for innocence, a crucifix, the stigmata, and a skull to suggest the passing of man's life. In 1929 he was made the patron saint of ecology.

CATHERINE
of ALEXANDRIA

PATRON SAINT of YOUNG WOMEN, MILLERS, PHILOSOPHERS, PREACHERS, SPINNERS, STUDENTS and WHEELWRIGHTS

IN 4th-century Alexandria, there lived a Christian noblewoman and philosopher of great beauty called Catherine. When she heard that the Roman emperor Maxentius was persecuting Christians, Catherine publicly protested. Astounded by her audacity, Maxentius sent fifty famous philosophers to try to change her mind, but Catherine, with her clever arguments, converted every one of them to Christianity. Maxentius immediately ordered their execution.

The emperor then tried to persuade Catherine to become his bride. Catherine refused, saying that she was already a bride of Christ. This answer drove Maxentius into a fury and he commanded that she be tortured on the infamous spiked wheel (later called the 'Catherine Wheel'). But angels are said to have thrown bolts of lightning so that the wheel broke and the spikes flew off, injuring onlookers but leaving Catherine unharmed. When she was eventually beheaded, milk not blood flowed from her neck, and angels carried her body up to Mount Sinai.

Catherine's symbols are a broken spiked wheel, a book of philosophy, a sword, a crown signifying her royalty and the palm leaf of martyrdom. All appear in this painting, in which the Spanish artist Yáñez portrays the saint as a graceful woman wearing a beautiful gown.

CHRISTOPHER

MANY legends surround Christopher, whose name in Greek means 'Christ-bearer'. According to one, he was a 3rd-century giant who worked as a ferryman, carrying travellers across a deep river.

One stormy day, Christopher heard a small child calling out to be carried across the river. Christopher lifted the child up on his shoulders, took his staff ~ an uprooted palm tree trunk ~ and set out across the water. The river rose higher and the child's weight grew heavier, until Christopher could hardly stand; but he struggled on to the opposite bank. He was astonished when the child said, "You have just carried the weight of the world." The child was Jesus, and the weight he spoke of was the sins of mankind. Jesus then told Christopher to plant his staff on the river bank, where it burst into leaf.

Christopher is pictured here by the artist Bouts, holding his symbol, a palm tree staff.

LUKE

PATRON SAINT of ARTISTS, BREWERS,
BUTCHERS, GLASSWORKERS, NOTARIES,
PAINTERS, DOCTORS and SURGEONS

ALMOST all we know about Luke comes from the New Testament. He was a Greek physician born at Antioch in Syria. He may have been an artist too, for according to legend he painted portraits of the Virgin Mary. But above all he was one of the four Evangelists, together with Matthew, Mark and John. (The word 'evangelist' in Greek means 'bringer of good news'.)

Luke's Gospel is remembered both for the many episodes describing how deeply Jesus cared for society's outcasts, and for its sympathetic view of women. Luke was a fine historian and writer: his second book, the Acts of the Apostles, records the missionary journeys he made with Paul during the Church's early years.

Here, Luke sits at his easel painting the Virgin Mary. The ox beside him symbolises his patience, strength and humanity.

JEROME

PATRON SAINT of LIBRARIANS and SCHOLARS

JEROME was one of the most studious of saints. Born in Dalmatia in the 4th century and educated in Rome, he studied the Classics, spoke Greek and Hebrew, wrote hundreds of learned letters and produced a standard Latin text of the Bible for Pope Damasus.

During his life Jerome made many enemies, for he was a fiery and argumentative priest. He spent five solitary years in the Syrian desert, eating only wild plants and honey, beating himself with stones and praying to God. He was a stern man, but there was a kind side to his nature. One day, a lion appeared outside his monastery, limping and growling with pain. Jerome showed no fear, but calmly dug out a huge thorn stuck deep in the poor beast's paw.

This painting shows how the grateful lion  became Jerome's loyal friend and his symbol. Jerome's other emblem, a red, tasselled cardinal's hat, lies nearby.

APOLLONIA

IN the year 249, a time when the Roman emperor Decius was persecuting Christians, a bloodthirsty mob in Alexandria decided to kill every Christian they could find. Many Christians fled, but Apollonia, a respected, elderly deaconess of the Church, stayed to comfort the Christians who remained.

The authorities arrested Apollonia and ordered her to worship their stone idols, but instead she made the sign of the Cross - which caused the statues to break into a thousand pieces. As a punishment, her teeth were pulled out one by one. Then she was dragged outside the city to a huge bonfire. She was told that unless she renounced her God, she would be thrown on to the fire. Apollonia decided that no one should have the pleasure of flinging her into the flames, so she pretended to need time to think. The crowd let her go for a moment and, to their astonishment, the old lady jumped straight on to the fire - so becoming a martyr and saint.

Whenever Apollonia is painted, she is shown either wearing a necklace of teeth or holding a single tooth in a pair of pincers. Her other symbol is a palm leaf, which stands for victory over death. Although Apollonia was an old woman at the time she died, most artists paint her as a young girl. Here, Zurbarán illuminates her portrait with gentle light and shadows, giving Apollonia an air of calm beauty.

POLO
NIA.

PAUL

PAUL, originally called Saul of Tarsus, was a Jew by birth, a tentmaker by trade, and a privileged Roman citizen. During his early life he hated Christians, and it is said that he took part in the stoning of Stephen, the first Christian martyr.

One day, Saul and his companions were on their way to Damascus to arrest Christians. Suddenly there was a flash of light from heaven. Saul fell to the ground, blinded, and heard a voice saying, "Saul, Saul, why persecutest thou me?" Saul asked who was speaking and the voice answered, "I am Jesus whom thou persecutest". Then the voice told him to go on to Damascus.

Saul, still unable to see, remained in Damascus for three days, until a Christian called Ananias restored his sight and baptised him. Saul changed his name to Paul, and went on to become one of the greatest of all Christian evangelists, making missionary journeys to Cyprus, Asia Minor and Greece; as a result, he became known as the Apostle of the Gentiles. His epistles have had a major influence on Christian teaching. Eventually he was imprisoned in Rome by the emperor Nero and executed in about 65 A.D. by the sword - which has become one of his emblems.

In Caravaggio's dramatically-lit painting, Saul has fallen under his horse and stretches out his arms towards the light that has blinded him. Beside him lies a sword; his other symbol is a book.

CECILIA

CECILIA, who lived in the 3rd century, was brought up as a Christian by her noble Roman father. On her wedding day, she converted her husband and his brother to Christianity, which angered the governor of Rome so much that he had the two men killed.

The governor ordered Cecilia to worship Rome's pagan gods and, when she refused, he sentenced her to be killed by suffocation in the bathroom of her own house. Miraculously, she survived. He then tried to have her beheaded with a sword. This time she survived for three days - long enough to give away all her wealth to the poor before she died.

Cecilia was said to be so close to heaven that she could hear the angels singing. She was not happy with her own musical skills, for she wanted to play the passionate songs that were in her heart. So she invented the organ, which came to represent harmony and praise for God. Since the 16th century she has been the patron saint of music.

In this three-quarter portrait by Pietro da Cortona, Cecilia wears a crown of fresh flowers to indicate her purity. She holds the palm leaf of martyrdom and her special symbol, the organ, stands in the background.

JOSEPH

PATRON SAINT of BELGIUM, CANADA, CHINA, PERU, BURSARS, CARPENTERS, the DYING, FATHERS and WORKING MEN

MOST of what we know about Joseph, husband of the Virgin Mary and foster-father of Jesus, is found in the New Testament Gospels. He was a poor carpenter born into a family descended from King David who married Mary and, after the birth of Jesus, became the protector of the Holy Family.

Soon after Jesus was born in Bethlehem, Joseph was warned in a dream to take his family to Egypt, because Herod, the king of Judea, was planning to kill the baby. Eventually, Joseph took the family back to Israel to live in Nazareth, where he continued to be a faithful guardian to Jesus and Mary, for he was a kind, dignified and practical man. Many hospitals and churches are named after him and the name Joseph is a popular Christian name.

Joseph's symbol of a budding staff comes from a legend that tells how, when the Virgin Mary was fourteen, each of her suitors left his staff at the temple, hoping a heavenly sign would favour one of them. The next morning, Joseph's staff budded into leaf and from it a dove flew up to heaven. Joseph's other symbols are his carpenter's tools, and a lily.

In this painting, the soft light of a candle held by a young child illuminates the face and hands of Joseph as he works at his trade, with all his carpenter's tools and pieces of wood scattered around him. There is a feeling of calm strength in Joseph's face and the artist conveys innocence and wonder in the gaze of the child, who might perhaps be the boy Jesus.

JOAN of ARC

ONE day in 1426, a 14-year-old French farmer's daughter called Joan had an amazing vision. In a blaze of light she heard the voices of saints telling her to save France from the English invaders.

Joan did not know how to ride or fight, yet she managed to persuade the Dauphin (later Charles VII) to let her lead a band of soldiers to Orléans to fight the English. Wearing white armour and carrying her own special banner, she rode in front of her troops and was wounded by an arrow in her chest – but won the battle! She even stood at the Dauphin's side with her banners in 1429 when he was crowned king, as this painting shows.

But Joan's popularity did not last long, for she was regarded with suspicion and jealousy by the court, the Church and the army. Eventually she was captured and sold to the English, who accused her of witchcraft. Finally, she was sentenced to be burnt at the stake, where she faced a horrible death with great courage. Although she died in 1431, aged only nineteen, she was not made a saint until 1920.

The French artist Ingres has painted Joan at the king's coronation wearing magnificent silver-grey battle dress. She stands proudly by the altar, on which we can see King Charles VII's golden crown. Covering the steps beside her is a blue and gold cloth patterned with fleur-de-lis, the lilies which are the emblem of Joan and also of the French kings.

INDEX of ARTISTS

FRONT COVER
and PAGE 25
**Saint Francis Preaching
to the Birds (detail)**
GIOTTO
about 1266-1337

Louvre, Paris

PAGE 10
**Saint John the Baptist
in Meditation (detail)**
HIERONYMOUS BOSCH
about 1450-1516

Museo Lazaro Gaudiano, Madrid

PAGE 13
**Saint John the Baptist and
Saint Mary Magdalen (detail)
Wing of a triptych**

HANS MEMLINC or MEMLING
about 1433-1494

Louvre, Paris

PAGE 9
**Saints Peter and Dorothy (detail)
Wing of an altarpiece**
MASTER of the
SAINT BARTHOLOMEW ALTARPIECE
active about 1470-1510

*Reproduced by courtesy of the Trustees,
The National Gallery, London*

PAGE 12
**Panel from The Virgin
and Child and Saints (detail)
'The Demidoff Altarpiece'**

CARLO CRIVELLI
active 1457-1493

*Reproduced by courtesy of the Trustees,
The National Gallery, London*

PAGE 15 and TITLE PAGE
**Saint Martin's
Renunciation of Arms
(detail)**

SIMONE MARTINI
about 1284-1344

S. Francesco, Assisi

and PAINTINGS

PAGES 16-17
**The Vision of
Saint Eustace (detail)**
PISANELLO
living 1395; died 1455(?)

*Reproduced by courtesy of the Trustees,
The National Gallery, London*

PAGE 18
Saint Lucy (detail)
FRANCESCO DEL COSSA
about 1435 - 1477

*National Gallery of Art, Washington
Samuel H. Kress Collection*

PAGE 21
**The Miraculous Draught
of Fishes (detail)**
RAPHAEL
1483-1520

*Victoria and Albert Museum,
London*

PAGE 22
**Saint George Slaying
the Dragon (detail)**
RAPHAEL
1483-1520

Louvre, Paris

PAGE 27
Saint Catherine (detail)
FERNANDO YÁÑEZ
DE LA ALMEDINA
active 1505-1536

Prado, Madrid

PAGE 28
Saint Christopher (detail)
Panel of a triptych
DIERIC BOUTS
about 1415-1475

Alte Pinakothek, Munich

PAGE 29
**Saint Luke Painting the Virgin
and Child (detail)**
Wing of an altarpiece
FOLLOWER OF MASSYS
early 16th century

*Reproduced by courtesy of the Trustees,
The National Gallery, London*

PAGES 30-31
Saint Jerome and the Lion (detail)
COLANTONIO
mid-15th century

Museo di Capodimonte, Naples

PAGE 33
Saint Apollonia (detail)
FRANCISCO DE ZURBARÁN
1598–1664
Louvre, Paris

PAGE 34
**The Conversion of
Saint Paul (detail)**
CARAVAGGIO
1571–1610
*Cerasi Chapel,
Sta. Maria del Popolo, Rome*

PAGE 37
Saint Cecilia (detail)
attributed to
PIETRO DA CORTONA
17th century
*Reproduced by courtesy of the Trustees,
The National Gallery, London*

PAGE 38
Saint Joseph the Carpenter (detail)
GEORGES DE LA TOUR
1593–1652
Louvre, Paris

PAGE 40
**Joan of Arc at the Coronation
of Charles VII (detail)**
JEAN-AUGUSTE-DOMINIQUE INGRES
1780–1867
Louvre, Paris

PHOTOGRAPHIC ACKNOWLEDGEMENTS

For permission to reproduce the paintings in this book and
for supplying photographs, the Publishers thank:

Bridgeman Art Library: 10, 21, 27
Giraudon/Bridgeman Art Library: front cover, 22, 25, 38
Lauros-Giraudon/Bridgeman Art Library: 40
The National Gallery, London: 9, 12, 16–17, 29, 37
© 1994 Board of Trustees, National Gallery of Art, Washington: 18, back cover
Scala: title page, 15, 28, 30–31, 33, 34
© R.M.N.: 13

CALENDAR of the PRINCIPAL FEASTS of SAINTS

✠ INDICATES SAINTS WHO ARE FEATURED IN THIS BOOK

JANUARY

1 Concordius
2 Basil the Great and Gregory of Nazianzus
3 Geneviève
4 Elizabeth Seton
5 Simeon Stylites
6 Balthasar, Caspar and Melchior
7 Raymund of Pennafort
8 Severinus of Noricum
9 Adrian of Canterbury
10 Marcian
11 Theodosius the Cenobiarch
12 Arcadius
13 Hilary of Poitiers
14 Sava of Serbia
15 Paul the Hermit
16 Marcellus I
17 Antony Abbot
18 Margaret of Hungary
19 Wulfstan
20 Sebastian
21 Agnes
22 Vincent of Saragossa
23 Ildefonsus
24 Francis of Sales
25 ✠ Conversion of Saint Paul
26 Paula
27 Angela Merici
28 Thomas Aquinas
29 Gildas
30 Bathildis
31 John Bosco

FEBRUARY

1 Brigid of Ireland
2 Joan de Lestonnac
3 Blaise
4 Andrew Corsini
5 Agatha
6 ✠ Dorothy
7 Luke the Wonderworker
8 Jerome Emiliani
9 ✠ Apollonia
10 Scholastica
11 Caedmon
12 Julian the Hospitaller
13 Catherine dei Ricci
14 Valentine
15 Sigfrid
16 Juliana
17 The Seven Servites
18 Fra Angelico
19 Conrad
20 Eleutherius
21 Fructuosus
22 Margaret of Cortona
23 Polycarp
24 Ethelbert
25 Walburga
26 Porphyry of Gaza
27 Gabriel Possenti
28 Oswald of Worcester
29 Cassian

MARCH

1 David of Wales
2 Chad
3 Cunegund
4 Casimir
5 Ciaran of Saighir
6 Colette
7 Perpetua and Felicitas
8 John of God
9 Frances of Rome
10 Forty Martyrs
11 Eulogius of Cordoba
12 Maximilian
13 Euphrasia
14 Matilda
15 Longinus
16 Heribert
17 Patrick
18 Edward the Martyr
19 ✠ Joseph
20 Cuthbert
21 Benedict
22 Deogratias of Carthage
23 Gwinear
24 Catherine of Vadstena
25 The Annunciation of the Blessed Virgin Mary
26 William of Norwich
27 Rupert of Salzburg
28 Alkelda of Middleham
29 Gwynllyw and Gwladys
30 John Climacus
31 Acacius

APRIL

1 Hugh of Grenoble
2 Mary of Egypt
3 Pancras of Taormina
4 Ambrose
5 Vincent Ferrer
6 Irenaeus of Sirmium
7 John Baptist de la Salle
8 Perpetuus
9 Madrun
10 Fulbert of Chartres
11 Stanislas
12 Zeno of Verona
13 Martin I
14 Caradoc
15 Paternus of Wales
16 Bernadette
17 Stephen Harding
18 Apollonius
19 Alphege
20 Agnes of Montepulciano
21 Anselm
22 Theodore of Sykeon
23 ✠ George
24 Fidelis of Sigmaringen
25 Mark
26 Stephen of Perm
27 Zita
28 Vitalis
29 Catherine of Siena
30 Pius V

MAY

1 Sigismund of Burgundy
2 Athanasius
3 Philip and James the Less
4 Florian
5 Hilary of Arles
6 Marian and James
7 John of Beverley
8 Peter of Tarentaise
9 Pachomius
10 Antoninus of Florence
11 Ignatius of Laconi
12 Nereus and Achilleus
13 Robert Bellarmine
14 Matthias
15 Isidore the Farmer
16 Brendan the Navigator
17 Paschal Baylon
18 Venantius
19 Dunstan
20 Bernardino of Siena
21 Godric
22 Rita of Cascia
23 Alexander Nevski
24 David of Scotland
25 Madeleine Barat
26 Augustine of Canterbury
27 Bede
28 Bernard of Aosta
29 Mary Magdalene de'Pazzi
30 ✠ Joan of Arc
31 Petronilla

JUNE

1 Justin
2 Erasmus
3 Martyrs of Uganda
4 Petroc
5 Boniface
6 Norbert
7 Meriadoc
8 William of York
9 Columba
10 Landry of Paris
11 Barnabas
12 Leo III
13 Antony of Padua
14 Methodius
15 Vitus
16 Cyricus and Julitta
17 Rainerius of Pisa
18 Gregory Barbarigo
19 Juliana Falconieri
20 Alban
21 Aloysius Gonzaga
22 John Fisher and Thomas More
23 Etheldreda
24 ✠ John the Baptist
25 William of Montevergine
26 John and Paul
27 Cyril of Alexandria
28 Potamiaena and Basilides
29 ✠ Peter and Paul
30 Martial of Limoges